•◦•○◦○ *BULLETPOINTS* ○◦○•◦•

OLYMPICS

Christopher Rigby

Miles Kelly
PUBLISHING

First published in 2004 by Miles Kelly Publishing Ltd
Bardfield Centre, Great Bardfield
Essex, CM7 4SL

2 4 6 8 10 9 7 5 3 1

Editor: Kate Miles

Design: Debbie Meekcoms

Picture Research: Liberty Newton

Production: Estela Godoy

British Library Cataloguing-in-Publication Data
A catalogue record for this book is available from the British Library

ISBN 1-84236-399-9

Printed in China

www.mileskelly.net
info@mileskelly.net

The publishers would like to thank the following artists and photographic agencies who have contributed to this book:
Richard Hook, John James, Guy Smith, Rudi Vizi
Page 7.OFF-DSK/AFP/GETTY IMAGES;8.STAFF-STF/AFP/GETTY IMAGES;
11 PATRICK HERTZOG-STF/AFP/GETTY IMAGES;17 JEAN-PIERRE MULLER-STF/AFP/GETTY IMAGES;
19 BENOIT-STF/AFP/GETTY IMAGES;20 JEFF HAYNES-STF/AFP/GETTY IMAGES;
23 OLIVIER MORIN-STF/AFP/GETTY IMAGES;24- GREG WOOD-STF/AFP/GETTY IMAGES;
27 PEDRO UGARTE-STF/AFP/GETTY IMAGES;29 OLIVER MULTHAUP-STF/AFP/GETTY IMAGES;
34 CORR-COR/AFP/GETTY IMAGES;35 RON KUNTZ-STF/AFP/GETTY IMAGES;
37 Bettmann/CORBIS;39 ARIS MESSINIS-STR/AFP/GETTY IMAGES.
All other photographs are from MKP archives; Corel, ILN,PhotoDisc.

Contents

Olympic origins

- **The ancient Olympics** took their name from the city of Olympia in the Greek district of Elis and were first contested in 776BC.

- **The games were originally held** in honour of the king of the Greek gods, Zeus. To commemorate them a gold and ivory statue of Zeus was erected in Zeus' temple in Olympia. This statue became one of the seven wonders of the ancient world.

- **The first 13 games** of the ancient Olympics consisted of just one event, a sprint race called the *stade* over a distance of 200 yards.

- **In the ancient Olympics** foreigners and slaves were not allowed to compete and women were forbidden from watching as the male athletes competed totally nude.

- **From the 6th century** BC women organized their own games. These were held in the city of Argos and called The Heraea after Hera, the wife of Zeus.

▲ *Prize-winning sporting heroes were rewarded with jars of olive oil or laurel wreaths.*

- **The ancient Olympics** were last held in AD393 and were subsequently abolished by the Christian Byzantine Emperor Theodosius I.

- **The modern Olympics** were the brainchild of a young French baron named Pierre de Coubertin. He believed that the revival of the games would help to restore the morale of his countrymen following their defeat in the Franco–Prussian War of 1870.

- **The first modern Olympics** were held in Athens in 1896. A total of 311 male athletes competed, 230 of these from Greece, representing just 14 different nations. The games were officially opened by King George of Greece on April 5.

- **In the 1896 games** the first placed athletes received a certificate, a silver medal and a crown of olive leaves.

- **The words of the Olympic creed** are attributed to Baron Pierre de Coubertin, who proclaimed: "The most important thing in the Olympic Games is not to win but to take part, just as the most important thing in life is not the triumph but the struggle. The essential thing is not to have conquered but to have fought well."

▶ *It is thought that this famous marble statue of a discus thrower is based on a bronze made by the sculptor Myron many centuries ago.*

5

On the track – 100 m to 400 m

- **The first ever event** contested at the modern Olympics of 1896 was a heat of the 100 m and it was won by the American sprinter Francis Lane in a time of 12.5 seconds.

- **In relay races**, the baton passed between the runners must be exchanged in a 20 m take-over zone. If the exchange takes place outside the zone the offending team is disqualified and placed last.

- **The achievements of the British Olympians** Harold Abrahams and Eric Liddell, who won the 100 m and 400 m gold in the 1924 games, were immortalized in the 1981 film *Chariots Of Fire*.

- **The 400 m and 400 m hurdles** are the longest track races to be run completely in lanes.

- **Starting blocks for sprinters** made their Olympic debut at the 1948 London games, which also witnessed the first ever photo finish. In the 100 m final the American athletes Harrison Dillard and Barney Ewell both crossed the finishing line in a time of 10.3 seconds. The judges awarded the race to Dillard after studying the photo print.

- **The hurdles used in Olympic events** have a maximum width of 1.2 m. Each hurdle weighs 10 kg and counterweights on their base prevent them from being blown over by strong winds.

- **At the 1968 Mexico City Olympics** the American sprinter Jim Hines was regaled as the fastest man on Earth after he became the first Olympian to run the 100 m in a time of less than 10 seconds.

▶ *The finalists for the 100 m race wait for the official to fire the starting gun at the 1896 games in Athens.*

- **The 1988 Olympic final** for the men's 100 m was billed as, 'The Race of the Century'. However the winner, Ben Johnson, was disqualified after failing a drugs test and the gold medal was awarded to Carl Lewis.

- **The world record for the men's 200 m** is 19.32 seconds and was set by Michael Johnson at the 1996 Atlanta games. The 200 m world record for women was set at the Seoul Olympics by Florence Griffith-Joyner in a time of 21.34 seconds.

- **At the 2000 Sydney Olympics** Marion Jones, representing the USA, became the first woman to win five track and field medals at the same games. She won gold in the 100 m, 200 m and 4 x 400 m relay, and bronze in the 4 x 100 m relay and the long jump.

On the track – 800 m to 10,000 m

▲ *Alberto Juantorena at the start of the men's 400 m event in 1976.*

● **The first women's 800 m Olympic event** was introduced at the 1928 games. However several competitors collapsed at the end of the event and as a result it was withdrawn and not reintroduced until 1960.

● **The bell used to signal** the last lap in long distance track events made its Olympic debut at the 1948 London games.

● **In the 3000 m steeplechase** the runners have to negotiate 28 barriers and seven water jumps.

● **The water in the water jump** of the 3000 m steeplechase has a depth of 0.71 m.

● **Cuban athlete Alberto Juantorena** is the only person in Olympic history to win the 400 m and 800 m at the same games, a feat he achieved at the 1976 Montreal Olympics.

● **Sebastian Coe is the only runner** to successfully defend a 1500 m Olympic title, winning his two gold medals in 1980 and 1984.

● **The 1984 women's 3000 m Olympic final** was marred with controversy when pre-race favourite Mary Decker fell after colliding with Zola Budd. The British contestant Budd eventually finished seventh but was booed for the remainder of the race.

▲ *Track athletes in the steeplechase race over obstacles including hurdles and water jumps.*

- **Runners have to complete** 25 laps of the track in the 10,000 m race.
- **Ethiopian runner Miruts Yifter** earned the nickname of Yifter the Shifter after winning gold medals in the 5000 m and 10,000 m at the 1980 Moscow Olympics.

> **. . .FASCINATING FACT. . .**
> In the 1972 games the Finnish athlete Lasse Viren won the gold medal for the 10,000 m, despite falling over in the race.

Field events – throwing

- **In Olympic events** the men's shot put weighs 7.26 kg and the women's shot weighs 4 kg.

- **British Olympic shot-putter Geoff Capes**, who retired in 1980, went on to be crowned The World's Strongest Man before becoming a leading breeder of budgerigars.

- **An aluminium javelin** was first used in the Olympic games in 1952.

- **The men's javelin weighs 800 g** and the women's javelin weighs 600 g.

- **Javelin thrower Tessa Sanderson** was the first British athlete to win an Olympic gold medal in a throwing event.

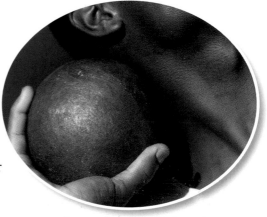

▲ *The term 'shot' derives from the Middle Ages when a cannon ball was sometimes used in place of a stone. Since 1896, shots are made of an amalgam of iron, bronze and lead.*

- **In the Olympics**, javelin throwers are allowed a run-up of 36.5 m before releasing the javelin from behind the throwing line.

- **At the 1956 games** Hal Connolly won the hammer gold medal for the United States despite the fact that his left arm was significantly shorter and less developed than his right arm.

- **For many years the hammer event** was exclusive to men. However at the 2000 Sydney games the women's hammer made its Olympic debut.

- **At the 1964 Olympics** Al Oerter discarded a neck brace protecting dislocated vertebra and produced what was then an Olympic record throw of 60.54 m for the discus.

- **The discus is the only field event** in which the women's world record betters that of the men's. This is largely due to the fact that the discus thrown by the women is half the weight of the men's.

▶ *French Olympic competitor Christophe Epalle swings the hammer during the 2000 Sydney Olympic Games.*

Field events – jumping

▲ *The Fosbury Flop has become a standard technique for high jumpers since Dick Fosbury modified the high jump by approaching the bar with his back to it in the early 1960s.*

- **Ancient Olympic competitors** were disqualified in the long jump events if they did not land entirely on their feet. To help them achieve greater distances the athletes held small weights in their hands called *halteres*.

- **In the 1900 Paris Olympics** Ray Ewry won gold medals for the standing jumps – high, long and triple despite being told as a young boy that he would never walk again due to polio.

- **At the 1968 Mexico games** the US athlete Dick Fosbury won the high jump gold medal, introducing a new style of jump that became known as the Fosbury Flop.

- **In high jump events** the height of the bar is raised by a minimum of 2 cm after each round of jumps.

- **US athlete Robert LeGendre** broke the world record for the long jump in 1924. He still only won a bronze medal as his record jump was part of a pentathlon competition in which he eventually finished third.

- **At the 1968 Mexico City Olympics** Bob Beamon recorded a long jump of 8.90 m on his way to winning the gold medal, breaking the previous world record by a staggering 55 cm.

- **The first ever winner of a gold medal** in the modern Olympics of 1896 was the triple jump champion James B Connolly of the United States.

- **At the 1964 Tokyo games** fibreglass poles were used for the first time in the pole vault events.

- **The box into which a pole vaulter** lodges his pole is 1 m long by 20 cm deep.

- **The Ukrainian-born Olympic gold medallist** Sergei Bubka was the first pole vaulter to clear a height of 6 m. In an outstanding career he broke the world record on 35 separate occasions.

▲ *The triple jump was originally called the hop, skip and jump. The athlete jumps from a take-off board and lands in sand.*

Gymnastics

▲ *The rings are the most physically demanding piece of gymnastic apparatus.*

- **The four disciplines in women's gymnastics** are the asymmetric bars, the vault, the beam and the floor.

- **The six disciplines in men's gymnastics** are the parallel bars, the vault, pommel horse, the rings, the high bar and the floor.

- **Rhythmic gymnastics**, involving the use of ropes, balls, clubs, hoops and ribbons made its Olympic debut in 1984 and is restricted to women.

- **The floor exercises** are performed on a square area that measures 12 m by 12 m.

- **The beam for the women's gymnastic** event has a width of just 10 cm.

- **The rings in men's gymnastics** stand 2.43 m above the floor on a 5.79 m frame.

- **Trampolining made its Olympic debut** at the 2000 Sydney games, despite the fact that the trampoline was invented in the 1930s by a carnival acrobat called George Nissan.

- **The greatest number of Olympic medals** won by one person is 18, a feat achieved by the Soviet gymnast Larissa Latynina between 1956 and 1964.

- **At the 1976 Montreal Olympics** the Romanian Nadia Comaneci became the first gymnast to score a perfect 10.

- **The only athlete to win eight medals** at one Olympic Games was the Soviet gymnast Aleksandr Dityatin, who achieved this feat in 1980. He was also the first male gymnast to score a perfect 10.

▲ *Elegance and style as well as timing and accuracy are important in gymnastics. Competitors are judged from the moment they step out to perform until they finish their routine.*

Equestrianism

- **The Olympic equestrian event** is divided into three categories – three day eventing, show jumping and dressage for both teams and individuals.

- **In the early days of the Olympic equestrian events**, only military officers were permitted to enter the three-day eventing competitions.

- **The individual dressage event** made its Olympic debut in 1912, but it took 60 years for a female rider to win the event when Liselott Linsenhoff won gold for Germany.

- **In the 1952 Olympic Games** the Danish rider Lis Hartel won a silver medal in the dressage event despite suffering from polio at the time.

- **In order to enter Olympic equestrian events** the horses must have their own valid passport as a means of identification.

- **At the 1956 Melbourne Olympics** all the equestrian events took place in the Swedish capital of Stockholm due to the strict quarantine laws of Australia.

- **Princess Anne represented Great Britain** at the 1976 Montreal Olympics and narrowly missed winning a bronze medal.

- **Lorna Johnstone, at the age of 70**, is the oldest-ever woman to compete in the Olympics. She was a member of the British equestrian squad at the 1972 Munich games.

- **In dressage events** only touch and pressure can be used to control the horses, whereas speaking to the horse or making noises leads to penalties.

... **FASCINATING FACT** ...
Equestrian events in the early days of the
modern Olympics included the high jump
and the long jump for horses.

▼ *On his way to winning a bronze medal, Saudi rider Khaled al-eid, jumps an obstacle on his horse* Khashm al-aan *at the 2000 Sydney Olympics.*

The marathon

▶ *Phedippides' run with news of the Athenians' victory over the Persians at Marathon gave rise to the introduction of the marathon race at the 1896 Olympic Games. The race's distance was standardized in 1908.*

- **The marathon was named after** a battle fought in 490BC in ancient Greece. A soldier named Phedippides ran to Athens with the news of a victory at the Battle of Marathon.

- **The first marathon at the modern Olympics** of 1896 was appropriately won by a Greek shepherd named Spiridon Louis, who was roared to victory by over 100,000 enthusiastic spectators.

- **Walking events in the Olympics** are contested over distances of 50 km and 20 km for men and 10 km for women.

- **The marathon is run over a distance of 42.195 km.** At the 1908 London games the extra 352 m was added in order that the finishing line faced the Royal Box.

- **The rules in walking races** state that competitors will be disqualified if they bend their knee from the time the leading foot hits the ground until it passes under the centre of the body.

- **The Ethiopian runner Abebe Bikila** won the marathon gold medal at the 1960 games running in his bare feet.

- **At the 1984 Los Angeles games** the American cyclist Connie Carpenter-Phinney became the first ever woman to win an Olympic gold medal for a cycling road race.

- **The first woman to win an Olympic gold medal** for the marathon was the American runner Joan Benoit who collected her title in 1984.

● **The opening event** of the 2004 Athens games is to be a cycle road race and the final event is the men's marathon.

● **The marathon in the** 2004 Athens games is to be contested on its historical course from the town of Marathonas to the finish at Panathinaoko Stadium in Athens.

◄ *American athlete Joan Benoit won the first Olympic women's marathon in 1984.*

19

Combat

● **Two styles of wrestling** are contested in the Olympic Games – Greco-Roman and freestyle.

● **The first martial art** to be included as a demonstration sport in the Olympics was savate, a French style of kick-boxing, demonstrated at the 1924 Paris Olympics.

● **Fencing is one of the few sports** that have been contested at every single Olympic Games. The swords used in Olympic competition are the foil, the épée and the sabre.

● **Mongolia has never won** an Olympic gold medal. It has however won five silver medals and eight bronzes, eight of these for wrestling.

▲ *British boxer Lennox Lewis, a former Olympic medal winner, raises his arms in victory after beating Mike Tyson in the World Heavyweight Championship fight in June 2002.*

- **At the 1964 Tokyo Olympics** the judo event made its debut at the specific request of the host nation.

- **Olympic boxing champions** who went on to become World Heavyweight Champions include Muhammed Ali, Joe Frazier, George Foreman and Lennox Lewis.

- **Boxers were first required** to wear protective head gear at the 1984 Olympics.

- **At the 1996 games** Kurt Angle won an Olympic gold medal for the United States at wrestling and went on to become the WWF World Champion.

- **At the 2000 Sydney Olympics,** Audley Harrison became the first British boxer since Chris Finnegan in 1968 to win an Olympic gold medal.

- **The International Olympic Committee** has given its approval to add women's wrestling to the programme for the 2004 Athens Games.

◄ Special protective equipment is necessary in fencing and tough clothing is worn. Even a blunt sword could cause injury.

'Athlons

- **The pentathlon** was added to the events of the ancient Olympics in 708BC and, according to legend, was instigated by Jason of Jason and the Argonauts fame.

- **The five events contested at the 708BC** games were the long jump, javelin, discus, foot race and wrestling. The contest was eventually won by Peleus, a close friend of Jason.

- **The modern pentathlon** comprises shooting, fencing, swimming, show jumping and a 3000 m running race.

- **In 1912 George Patton** represented the United States in the pentathlon and famously went on to serve as a general in World War II.

- **In 1912 the American athlete** Jim Thorpe won both the pentathlon and decathlon gold medals. The governing body later withdrew his medals after it was discovered that he played baseball professionally.

- **The first event of the decathlon** is a 100 m track race and the final event is a 1500 m track race.

- **The only athletes** to win two Olympic golds in the decathlon are Bob Mathias of the United States in 1948 and 1952 and Daley Thompson of Great Britain in 1980 and 1984.

- **The triathlon event** consists of a 10 km run, a 1.5 km swim and a 40 km cycle race.

- **The seven events** contested in the women's heptathlon are the long jump, the high jump, javelin, shot put, 100 m hurdles, 200 m and 800 m.

▶ *British athlete Denise Lewis soars through the air in the heptathlon long jump at the Sydney 2000 Olympics.*

...FASCINATING FACT...
The decathlon takes its name from the Greek words for 'ten' and 'contest'.

In the water

- **The men's water polo event** made its Olympic debut in 1900, but the women's water polo competition had to wait a further 100 years before its introduction at the 2000 Sydney Olympics.

- **Swimming** events at the 1900 Paris Olympics included an underwater swim that took place in the River Seine.

- **Johnny** Weissmuller, who went on to play Tarzan in 19 films, won four Olympic gold medals for swimming and a bronze medal for water polo.

- **Australian swimmer Dawn Fraser** is the only woman to have won 100 m gold medals in consecutive Olympics. In 1962 she became the first woman to swim 100 m in under one minute.

- **In synchronized swimming** Olympic events the pool must be at least 3 m deep and the water temperature is set at 26°C, plus or minus one degree.

- **Greg Louganis,** the most successful diver in Olympic history, won his last gold medal in 1988, despite cutting his head open after striking the spring board.

- **The Danish sailor Paul Elvstrom** enjoyed an Olympic career that spanned 40 years from 1948 to 1988 and won gold medals in four consecutive Olympics.

- **Ian Thorpe, nicknamed Thorpedo,** won three swimming gold medals at the 2000 Sydney Olympics at the tender age of 17.

- **At the 2000 Sydney Olympics** Birgit Fischer of Germany won two gold medals in the kayak event and became the first ever woman to win medals 20 years apart.

◀ *Olga Brusnikina and Maria Kisseleva, Russian synchronized swimmers, perform their duet technical routine at the Sydney 2000 Olympics.*

> **. . . FASCINATING FACT . . .**
> At the 1992 Barcelona Games the Spanish cox in the rowing eights was an 11-year-old boy named Carlos Front.

Olympic ball sports

- **Tennis was contested in every Olympic Games** from 1896 to 1924 and was then removed from the programme before being reintroduced in 1988.

- **At the 1988 games** Steffi Graff became the first tennis player to win a Golden Slam, consisting of the US Open, the Australian Open, the French Open, Wimbledon and an Olympic gold medal.

- **Due to the mass boycott** of the 1980 Moscow Olympics, only two teams competed in the women's hockey tournament, with Zimbabwe beating the Soviet Union to win the gold medal.

▲ *In baseball, each fielder wears a mitt. The ball is hard and covered with white-coloured cowhide.*

- **The most successful nation** in Olympic men's hockey is India, winning a total of eight gold medals in the 20th century.

- **Croquet** made its only Olympic appearance at the 1900 games in Paris.

- **Great Britain won** the first gold medals for men's football in 1908 and 1912.

- **Currently, Olympic men's football teams** are allowed to include professional footballers with an age limit of 23, with each team allowed to field three over-age players.

- **Women's football** made its Olympic debut in 1996, and a world-record crowd for a women's sporting event of 76,000 watched the United States beat China in the final.

- **Baseball first achieved medal status** at the 1992 Olympics, with Cuba winning gold.

- **The USA's gold medal** winning basketball team at the 1992 Olympics became known as the Dream Team and included the stars Michael Jordan and Magic Johnson.

▲ *Germany v Brazil in the women's bronze medal soccer game at the Sydney 2000 games.*

Winter Olympics

- **Eighteen Winter Olympics** were held in the 20th century, the first in 1924 in France and the last in 1998 in Japan.

- **The 2002 Winter Olympics** at Salt Lake City had three official mascots. They were a bear called Coal, a coyote called Copper and a hare called Powder.

- **No country in the Southern Hemisphere** has ever hosted the Winter Olympics.

- **The Winter Olympics** have been hosted by the United States on several occasions. In 1932 and 1980 they were held at Lake Placid, New York; in 1960 they took place at Squaw Valley, California; and in 2002 at Salt Lake City, Utah.

- **At the 2002 Winter Olympics** the Canadian team won the gold medal for ice hockey beating their fierce rivals, the United States, 5–2 in the final.

- **The Salt Lake City Winter Olympics** set the record for being the games held at the highest-ever altitude, at over 1300 m above sea level.

- **At the 1980 Winter Olympics,** the American speedskater Eric Heiden became the first-ever person to win five individual gold medals at a single games.

- **Up to and including the 2002 games,** Norway has won the greatest number of Winter Olympic gold medals with a total of 94. In this time Great Britain has won just eight gold medals.

- **The Great Britain and Northern Ireland** women's curling team became national heroes in 2002 when they won the Olympic gold medal, beating Switzerland 4–3 in the final.

- **The 2006 Winter Olympics** are to be held in the Italian city of Turin. The last time Italy hosted the games was in 1956 at the venue of Cortina d'Ampezzo. This venue inspired the name of the Ford *Cortina* car.

▶ *The gold medal-winning German ski-jumping team celebrate on the podium at the 2002 Salt Lake City Winter Olympics.*

Summer Olympics

▲ *The last pure gold Olympic medals were awarded in 1912.*

- **At the first modern Summer Olympics** held in 1896 in Athens, 311 male athletes took part and not one female.

- **In 1916, 1940 and 1944** the Summer Olympics were cancelled due to World Wars I and II.

- **The opening ceremony** of the Olympics is always led by Greece, with the host nation marching out last.

- **Gold medallists** for the United Kingdom at the 2000 Olympics included Jason Queally for cycling, Denise Lewis for the heptathlon, Steve Redgrave for rowing, Iain Percy for sailing, Jonathan Edwards for the triple jump and Audley Harrison for boxing.

- **The first Summer Olympics** to be televised live were the 1960 games hosted by Rome.

- **Recent events** that have been added to the Olympic programme include beach volleyball and mountain biking in 1996 and tae kwan do and women's weightlifting in 2000.

- **The term Olympiad** derives from the Greek language and means every four years.

- **Olympic athletes** were first tested for anabolic steroids at the 1976 games in Montreal, Canada.

- **The tug-of-war** was an Olympic event from 1900 to 1920. In 1908 a team of London policemen won the gold medal.

● **Venues for the modern Olympics were:** 1896 – Athens, Greece; 1900 – Paris, France; 1904 – St Louis, USA; 1908 – London, UK; 1912 – Stockholm, Sweden; 1920 – Antwerp, Belgium; 1924 – Paris, France; 1928 – Amsterdam, Holland; 1932 – Los Angeles, USA; 1936 – Berlin, Germany; 1948 – London, UK; 1952 – Helsinki, Finland; 1956 – Melbourne, Australia; 1960 – Rome, Italy; 1964 – Tokyo, Japan; 1968 – Mexico City, Mexico; 1972 – Munich, Germany; 1976 – Montreal, Canada; 1980 – Moscow, USSR; 1984 – Los Angeles, USA; 1988 – Seoul, South Korea; 1992 – Barcelona, Spain; 1996 – Atlanta, USA; 2000 – Sydney, Australia; 2004 Athens, Greece.

▼ *Athens, the capital of Greece, dominated by the Acropolis, host of the 2004 Olympic Games.*

Olympic milestones

- **In 1900** the Middlesex-born Charlotte Cooper became the first female to win an Olympic gold medal after winning the tennis tournament.

- **Electronic timing equipment** for track races was used for the first time in the Olympics at the 1912 Stockholm games.

- **The Olympic motto** *Citius, Altius, Fortius* meaning 'Swifter, Higher, Stronger' was introduced at the 1920 Olympics.

- **The Olympic flag** of five interlocking rings representing the five participating continents was introduced at the 1920 Antwerp games.

- **At the 1928 games** in Amsterdam, the tradition of releasing doves to symbolize peace between the nations was introduced.

- **The Olympic torch** was first carried from Olympia to the games venue at the 1936 Berlin games.

- **Sex testing was introduced** at the 1968 Mexico Olympics after questions were raised in the 1950s and 1960s as to the true sex of certain female competitors.

▲ *At least one of the colours of the Olympic rings is represented in the flag of every participating nation.*

- **The 1972 Munich Olympics** witnessed the first official Olympic mascot in the form of a dachshund called Waldi.

- **The 1980 Moscow Olympics** were boycotted by the United States and over 30 other nations in protest against the Soviet Union's 1979 invasion of Afghanistan.

- **The new Olympic stadium** built for the 2000 Sydney Olympics had a capacity of 110,000 and cost $690 million to build.

▼ *The opening ceremony of the 1936 Berlin Olympics. The stadium held 110,000 spectators.*

Olympic hall of fame

- **Paavo Nurmi** – Nicknamed the Flying Finn, Nurmi won nine gold medals in the 1920s including a 1500 m and 5000 m-race with only one hour between each race.

- **Mildred Babe Didrikson** – The legendary US athlete is considered by many to be the greatest all-round sports star ever. She won Olympic golds in the high hurdles and the javelin and after the Olympics became the US National Golf Champion.

- **Jesse Owens** – Born James Cleveland, the German dictator Adolf Hitler infamously refused to shake the hand of Owens after he had won four gold medals at the 1936 Berlin Olympics.

▲ *US athlete Jesse Owens, winner of four Olympic gold medals in 1936.*

- **Fanny Blankers-Koen** – The Dutch athlete won four gold medals at the 1948 Olympics when she was 30 years old and the mother of two children.

- **Emil Zatopek** – In 1956 the Czech athlete became the only person to win gold medals for the 5000 m, the 10,000 m and the marathon at the same games.

- **Mark Spitz** – US swimmer Spitz won seven gold medals at the 1972 games, a feat all the more remarkable in that he won them all in a world record time.

- **Carl Lewis** – The US athlete won a career total of nine Olympic gold medals in the long jump and sprint events and in 1980 emulated his hero Jesse Owens by winning four gold medals at one games.

- **Florence Griffith-Joyner** – Affectionately known as Flo-Jo, this popular US athlete won three sprint golds at the 1988 Olympics but tragically died ten years later aged 38.

- **Steve Redgrave** – The British rower is the only rower to win gold medals at five consecutive Olympics, winning his fifth at the 2000 Sydney Olympics.

▲ *US athlete Florence Griffith-Joyner crosses the finishing line in the 1988 Seoul Olympics.*

Strange but true

- **At the 1900 Paris Olympics** no medals were awarded to the winners. Instead valuable pieces of art were presented to the victorious athletes.

- **In 1904** at the St Louis Olympics, the American gymnast George Eyser won six medals despite the fact that his left leg was made of wood.

- **The 1908 games** due to be held in the city of Rome were moved to London following the eruption of the volcano Vesuvius.

- **The oldest individual** to win an Olympic medal was 72-year-old Oscar Swahm, who won a shooting silver medal for Sweden in 1920.

- **The continents of South America and Africa** have to date never hosted the Olympic Games.

- **The Olympic flame** in Greece is rekindled every two years using the sun's rays and a reflective mirror.

- **In 1980 Stella Walsh**, who won the women's 100 m gold medal at the 1932 games, was accidentally killed in a Cleveland parking lot during a robbery. An autopsy revealed that the Polish-born athlete was actually a man.

- **The five colours of the Olympic rings** of blue, black, red, yellow and green were chosen because at least one of these colours is represented in the flag of every participating nation.

- **The oldest-ever person** to carry the Olympic torch was Jade Lockett, a 109-year-old Australian who carried the torch for a distance, prior to the 2000 Sydney Olympics.

> **. . . FASCINATING FACT . . .**
> Olympic gold medals contain just 1 g
> of gold and 210 g of silver.

▶ *Stella Walsh, photographed in 1930, was winner of the gold medal for the women's 100 m at the 1932 games. It was much later revealed that she was in fact a man. Sex testing on athletes was introduced at the time of the 1968 Mexico Olympics after the true sexual identity of athletes had long been an issue.*

Preparations for the 2004 games

- **The 2004 Olympic Games** to be held in Athens are the 28th games of the modern Olympics.

- **Athens** beat off rival bids from Buenos Aires, Cape Town, Istanbul, Lille, Rio, Rome, St Petersburg, San Juan, Seville and Stockholm to host the 2004 games.

- **Some 10,500 athletes and 5500 team officials** from 210 national Olympic committees are to participate in the 2004 games.

- **The Olympic village** for the 2004 games has been built 11 km from the Olympic stadium and contains 2292 homes with the capacity to house over 17,000 athletes. The estimated cost of the village is $300 million.

- **More than 8000 volunteer performers** and 2000 artistic and technical volunteers are needed for the opening and closing ceremonies of the 2004 games.

- **To ensure the smooth running of the games** an estimated 45,000 security personnel are to be employed including 25,000 police officers.

- **Official mascots for the 2004 games** are a pair of brother and sister dolls called Phevos and Athena, inspired by a 7th century BC Greek doll, to symbolize brotherhood among all people.

- **The official emblem of the 2004 games** is a white olive wreath on a blue background to symbolize the sacred tree of Athens and the traditional colours prevalent in the Greek countryside.

- **The official opening ceremony** is to take place in the Olympic stadium in Athens on August 13, 2004 with the closing ceremony on August 29, 2004.

▲ *The new tennis centre (bottom right) and Olympic stadium (top) under construction.*

Index

40